DREAMGIRLS

Based on the novelization by Denene Millner

Screenplay by Bill Condon

LEVEL 3

SCHOLASTIC

Adapted by: Patricia Reilly

Publisher: Jacquie Bloese

Commissioning Editor: Helen Parker

Editors: Jo Spencer and Helen Parker

Cover layout: Emily Spencer

Designer: Victoria Wren

Picture research: Emma Bree

Photo credits: Front cover image and internal photos © 2006 by DreamWorks LLC and Paramount Pictures. All rights reserved.
Page 5: C. Rotkin/Corbis.
Page 15: Bettmann/Corbis.
Pages 16 & 17: J. Collins/Alamy; Bettman/Corbis.
Page 20: G. Hohenberg/Alamy.
Page 52: Bettmann/Corbis.
Pages 64 & 65: P. Burnett/AP/PA; J. Kimura, P. Kramer, E. Agostini, V. Bucci, B. Bedder/Getty Images.
Pages 66 & 67: M. Kappeler/AFP/Getty Images; G. Hershorn/Reuters/Corbis.
Pages 68 & 69: Bettmann, B. Smith/Corbis; A. Quinn/AP/PA; Pictorial Press Ltd/Alamy.

Published by arrangement with HarperCollins Publishers, New York, New York, USA

Mary Glasgow Magazines (Scholastic Ltd.)
Euston House
24 Eversholt Street
London
NW1 1DB

Printed in Singapore. Reprinted 2008.

CONTENTS

DREAMGIRLS

Lorrell sings back-up in the group, the Dreamettes.
Effie is the lead singer of the Dreamettes. She has a strong and amazing voice.
Deena sings back-up in the Dreamettes. Like her best friends, Effie and Lorrell, she wants to be a star.

C.C. is Effie's brother. He writes all the songs and plans the dances for the Dreamettes.

Jimmy Early is a famous R&B singer from Detroit. His music is very successful in the black music charts.

Marty is Jimmy Early's manager. He thinks Jimmy belongs to him.

Curtis manages a garage and sells Cadillac cars. He wants to become a manager in the music business.

PLACES

Detroit is in the north of the USA, near the Great Lakes. A Frenchman called Antoine de Cadillac founded the city in 1701. The Cadillac car was named after him. Detroit is sometimes known as the 'Motor City' because of all the car factories there.

The Detroit Theatre has a show with black music artists once a week. It's called the 'Motor City Show'. Once a year, the theatre also has a talent show.

DREAMGIRLS

CHAPTER 1
A chance to be famous

'Hurry up, Effie!' Deena shouted as she ran towards the theatre.

'I'm going as fast as I can. It isn't easy to run in these shoes,' Effie cried. 'Anyway, it's not *my* fault we're late. We were waiting for *your* mother to go to sleep before we could leave!'

Effie was a long way behind Deena and their other friend, Lorrell. Effie's brother, C.C., was following, too. He wrote all their songs and planned their dances.

The three best friends were going to the Motor City Show at the Detroit Theatre. It was every Monday night, and it was the only night black people were allowed into the theatre. Everybody wanted to go. Even R&B* stars like Jimmy Early played there.

Early was from Detroit, but now he was a big star. Once a year, the theatre had a talent show.

Lorrell reached the theatre first and smiled as she read the sign: TONIGHT JIMMY EARLY AND TALENT SHOW.

Tonight was the three girls' big chance. They had started singing together when they were children. Now they sang as a group called the Dreamettes. They hoped to win the talent show tonight. They wanted to become stars. But they were nearly an hour late.

♫ ♫ ♫

* *R&B is a style of black music.*

Deena ran past Lorrell towards the back door of the theatre. The door opened and two women came out. They were angry. Jimmy Early's manager, Marty, was following them.

'Come back, ladies! Please! Jimmy needs you tonight!'

'No way – we're finished! Find someone else!' said one of the women. They got into a taxi and left.

'What am I going to do?' said Marty. He walked past Deena, back into the theatre. He looked very worried.

A handsome man in a suit was standing by the door. He'd also seen what had happened with the two women. An idea came to him.

Deena went inside the theatre. 'Come on!' she shouted to Effie and Lorrell. 'We'll be too late!'

'Hi. I'm Curtis Taylor,' the man said. But Deena didn't really hear him. She was looking at Oak, the talent show organiser.

'Look, I know we're late,' she began.

'Who are you?' Oak asked impatiently.

'Deena Jones,' she said. 'I'm one of the Dreamettes.'

Oak looked at his list. 'You're late.'

'I know,' Deena said, 'but–'

'Bad luck. The show's over,' Oak said. He turned away, but Curtis stopped him.

'Brother,' Curtis said quietly, 'I can see you're a good man. So why not give these girls a chance?'

Oak looked at Curtis. 'OK,' he said finally. 'They can sing last. After Tiny Joe Dixon.'

'Oh, thank you!' Deena smiled, and the girls ran to get ready.

♫ ♫ ♫

Wearing their best dresses, the girls waited at the side of the stage for Tiny Joe Dixon to finish his act.

'And now, please welcome our final act, the lovely … Creamettes,' the presenter said.

'It's the *Dream*ettes! The *Dream*ettes!' Deena shouted as they ran onto the stage.

The band started playing and the heavy curtains opened. When she saw all the people in the crowd, Lorrell couldn't move. Deena took her hand and together they moved to the music. Then Effie began to sing; her voice was amazing.

When Effie finished the song, the crowd went wild. They were still shouting for the girls when all the other musicians came back on stage. Everyone thought the girls would win.

'Now remember, the winner of the talent show will perform here at the Detroit Theatre for seven nights,' the presenter was saying. 'And that very talented Star of Tomorrow is … Tiny Joe Dixon!'

Everybody was surprised, and the girls were very disappointed. They felt it was the end of all their dreams.

'Come on,' Effie said sadly. 'Let's go home. We aren't going to be famous now.'

Just then, Curtis walked over. 'You girls need a break, and I'm here to give it to you,' he said. 'You can have thirty dollars each to sing with Jimmy Early tonight.'

'Jimmy Early!' Lorrell cried. 'But he's really famous! Do you mean it?'

'Yes,' said Curtis. 'And,' he continued, 'Jimmy would also like you to go on a ten-week tour with him, starting tomorrow.'

'Oh!' Deena cried. 'Effie, can you believe it? We're going to sing back-up for Jimmy Early!'

'I don't do back-up,' Effie said angrily.

'Effie,' Lorrell said, 'this could be our big break.'

Curtis moved over to Effie.

'You're talented, and you're beautiful,' he said. 'But that isn't enough. You need a break. Take this chance, and I'll look after you, I promise. I'll be your manager. And believe me, I won't disappoint you.'

'Please, Effie,' Deena said.

Everybody waited. Effie was thinking about it. Then suddenly she shouted, 'OK! Our manager says we're singing behind Jimmy Early tonight!'

Deena and Lorrell were so happy. Curtis smiled. Now he had a back-up group for Jimmy Early. He went to find Marty and tell him the good news.

♫ ♫ ♫

'Are you ready for Jimmy Early?' the presenter cried. The crowd started to shout.

In his dressing room, Jimmy stood up and put on his jacket.

'Look, I've found a fantastic group of three girls who can sing back-up tonight,' Marty told him.

'Three? I only need two,' Jimmy said.

'OK then, two,' Marty agreed. 'Let's go.'

Curtis was waiting outside. He knew that if this worked, his dream might finally come true. He'd wanted to be a music manager since he was twelve years old. He'd tried writing his own songs and he'd even married a singer. Now, he was managing her father's Cadillac sales business. But he'd never given up his music dreams – and now he had a chance.

'Jimmy wants two girls,' Marty said to Curtis.

'Two? Wait a minute. This is a group,' Curtis said. He tried to stay calm.

'Sorry, brother. It's two or nothing,' Marty said. And he led Jimmy towards the stage.

'Then it's nothing,' Curtis said.

Just then Jimmy saw the three girls on stage. He smiled when he saw Lorrell. She smiled back at him. She couldn't believe she was meeting a real star!

'It's OK. Three's fine,' Jimmy called to Marty. 'Ladies, you are saving my life! I'll do anything for you,' he said and took Lorrell's hand. He looked into her eyes. 'What do you want?'

'Well, Mr Early … you could teach us the song,' Lorrell said shyly.

Jimmy laughed. 'OK,' he said. 'That's easy.'

He started to sing, and the girls soon learned the words. They loved singing with Jimmy, and Jimmy thought they were great.

♫ ♫ ♫

The curtains opened and the concert started. Jimmy flew across the stage on his knees, screaming all the way. And when he started to sing the crowd went wild. He jumped up and turned as the musicians danced and played behind him.

The Dreamettes were nervous, but they were excited,

too. Here they were, on stage, with Jimmy Early! They couldn't believe it. Was this their big break?

CHAPTER 2
The hit

The next morning, Deena and Lorrell were standing outside Effie's house. They had their suitcases with them.

'Effie, the bus will be here soon!' Lorrell shouted. 'Hurry up!'

They couldn't go without Effie. She was their best friend, and she was the lead singer. Deena and Lorrell had always sung back-up, and they were happy to do that. Effie had an amazing voice. She was the real star of the show.

Finally, a minute before the bus arrived, Effie ran out of her house, followed by C.C., her brother. The three girls jumped onto the bus.

'Make me proud of you!' C.C. shouted to his sister as the bus left.

'I will,' Effie promised.

♫ ♫ ♫

The girls were very excited about being on tour, but they soon discovered that it wasn't easy for black people. Often they had to wait in 'coloured* only' rooms before they went on stage. Even Jimmy, the star, found it hard sometimes to get a drink or a meal before the show. But the moment Jimmy walked on stage and started his act, the crowd always went wild. Jimmy's show was hot.

Soon Jimmy and the girls became a team, and he thought they were all great. But he had a special smile for Lorrell. She liked Jimmy, too. She tried to sing her best all the time. She wanted him to notice her.

♫ ♫ ♫

* *'Coloured' was another word for 'black people'. At this time (the early 1960s) black and white people weren't allowed to mix in most public places.*

One night, they were all on the tour bus. As usual, the men were at the back and the girls were at the front. Curtis's Aunt Ethel was on tour with them and wouldn't let the girls sit with the men. But Lorrell wanted to sit next to Jimmy, so she waited until Aunt Ethel was asleep. Then she walked quietly to the back of the bus and sat next to him.

'Oh, Mr Early,' she said, 'I can't believe this is really happening to me. I can't believe I'm your back-up singer! It's so exciting!'

'Jimmy, baby. Call me Jimmy.'

'Oh … Jimmy,' Lorrell laughed. 'You're so crazy.'

Jimmy took her hand. Lorrell smiled.

Jimmy tried to kiss her, but she stopped him. 'Are you married?' she asked.

Jimmy looked surprised. 'Yeah. Everyone knows I'm married!' he said.

Lorrell stopped smiling. 'Well, get your married hands off me!' she said, and she got up and walked quickly back to her seat.

♫ ♫ ♫

Deena and Effie were sitting at a table in the 'Blue Bleu' club in Detroit. They had just finished their last concert on the tour with Jimmy. Deena was giving Effie some advice.

'I'm just saying, you might do better with boys if you were a bit more … um …' Deena stopped.

'Shy? Sweet, like you?' Effie laughed.

'Well, boys like it,' Deena replied.

'I'm not interested in *boys*, Deena. I prefer *men*.' Effie watched Curtis walk over to their table.

'What are you two talking about?' he asked.

Effie smiled. 'Well, Curtis,' Effie said, 'we were wondering … are you married?'

Curtis didn't move. 'I was married,' he said. 'It didn't work out.'

'So,' Effie continued, 'do you like thin girls like Deena, or real women?'

'Effie!' Deena cried.

Just then C.C. walked over.

'I'll answer you in a minute, ladies,' Curtis said. He turned to C.C. 'Are you ready?'

'Sure,' C.C. said.

♫ ♫ ♫

'It's not working, Marty,' Jimmy said. 'I'm not as good as I was. What's wrong?'

'But you were great tonight,' Marty said.

'No,' Jimmy shook his head. 'I need something, man. Something new.'

Curtis and C.C. walked up.

'You need a new sound,' Curtis said. 'Jimmy, you remember Effie's brother, C.C. He's a very talented young writer.'

'Oh yeah,' Jimmy said. 'You wrote that song the girls sang at the talent show.'

'Yes,' C.C. said proudly.

'What do you think of that song, Marty?' Jimmy asked. Jimmy had a look in his eye.

'Well, it's kind of –' Marty began.

'Boring?' Jimmy finished.

'Yes,' said Marty. 'It's boring.'

They smiled at C.C., but it wasn't a nice smile. C.C. was angry and upset, and he walked away. Curtis didn't leave, though. He wanted to be Jimmy's manager. He wanted to have a hit song that would put Jimmy in the pop charts.

'There's got to be a way to bring our music to more people,' Curtis said to Jimmy. 'Only this time, with our artists. Our money. We can do it, together. I can do it. Trust me.'

Jimmy laughed, but then he stopped. C.C. was singing.

'Got me a Cadillac, Cadillac, Cadillac … Got me a Cadillac car,' C.C. sang. Then the girls started singing back-up. It sounded amazing. Jimmy was interested.

A Cadillac car from the early 1960s

'Don't listen to them, Jimmy. You're a star already! You've got a recording contract,' Marty said. He didn't want Curtis to steal Jimmy from him.

'A recording contract? It's a joke!' said Curtis. 'That contract is with a weak label, and if Jimmy stays with them, he'll never be a real star. He'll never get into the pop charts.'

Jimmy was listening. Marty looked cross. Curtis looked into Jimmy's eyes.

'One record, that's all I'm asking. What have you got to lose?'

♫ ♫ ♫

The next day, Jimmy and the girls recorded *Cadillac Car*. They used the garage where Curtis sold Cadillacs as a studio. Two nights later Curtis, C.C. and Wayne, Curtis's assistant, put the first boxes of records into Curtis's car. 'Rainbow Records', the label said. It was the name Curtis had chosen for his music business. They drove to WAMK, a local radio station. Curtis was sure the DJ would play the record when he'd heard it.

♫ ♫ ♫

'Curtis, why are we driving around like this?' Effie asked. She was sitting in the back of the car with Deena and Lorrell. Curtis and C.C. were in front. Curtis didn't answer; he just turned up the radio.

Suddenly the DJ said, 'This is Jimmy Early's new sound, and I think you're going to enjoy it.' Then their song, *Cadillac Car*, started playing!

'Curtis, we're on the radio!' Effie cried excitedly. The girls couldn't believe it. They were stars!

And that was the start of their climb up the charts. The record went to number eight on the R&B charts and number thirty-eight on *Billboard's** pop charts.

It was an unbelievable hit for a black artist.

They really were stars.

Records were like this in the 1960s.

* Billboard *is a music magazine. It has weekly pop charts that show how successful a song is in the USA.*

CHAPTER 3
Steppin' to the Bad Side

C.C. threw a glass at the TV.

'C.C!' Effie cried.

'Effie, that white boy's singing my song. *My* song!' C.C. shouted. 'I can't believe this!'

They were watching *American Bandstand*, one of the most popular music programmes in America. The guests on the show were Dave and the Sweethearts – a very blond, very white group that often appeared in *Billboard*. Their records were often played on radio stations. And now Dave and the Sweethearts were on TV singing their new song, *Cadillac Car*. They'd stolen the song from Jimmy and the girls, and changed the style. Now it was sweet and slow, so that white people would like it.

American Bandstand was a popular music show in the 1960s.

C.C. was angry. He was so angry that he couldn't even sit down.

'Don't get upset, C.C.,' said Effie. 'Someone's going to

pay for this – they can't just steal our song.' But C.C. knew it wasn't true. Often no one did anything when white people stole things from black people. In the early 1960s some people didn't even think it was stealing. C.C. ran out of the door.

♫ ♫ ♫

'How can they do that? It's my song, Curtis!' C.C. shouted. Curtis didn't answer. He looked angry.

'Marty says it happens all the time,' Wayne said.

'Why didn't Marty protect us? They stole our hit!' C.C. cried.

'Forget Marty. I'm going to protect the band now,' Curtis said slowly.

'Go home, C.C. Write a new song. And come back here early tomorrow morning – we've got work to do.'

C.C. didn't know what Curtis was talking about, but he didn't ask any questions. He needed somebody to protect his songs – somebody strong, like Curtis. He went home and worked on his song all night. It was called *Steppin' to the Bad Side* and he knew it was a hit.

♫ ♫ ♫

C.C. noticed the sign first. It said: SALE – EVERYTHING MUST GO. He walked into the car showroom.

'OK, C.C.,' said Curtis. 'I'll tell you what you're going to do. You're going to sell all these cars in the next ten days.'

'But – that's crazy! What about your car business? You can't sell everything!' said C.C.

'Music is my business now,' Curtis said. 'And we can't make music here at Rainbow Records if we have to sell cars too.'

C.C. couldn't believe it. Curtis was amazing. He loved music and he said C.C.'s songs were great. He'd helped to get C.C.'s hit record on the radio. And now C.C. could see that Curtis had even bigger plans for the future. C.C. smiled at his new boss and went out into the car showroom.

♫ ♫ ♫

It took them seven days to sell all the cars. As the last car left, Curtis turned on a new sign. It lit up: RAINBOW RECORDS – THE SOUND OF TOMORROW.

Curtis counted up the money from the cars and put it in a big bag. 'Come on, let's go,' he said to C.C.

'Where are we going? The banks are closed!' said C.C.

'We aren't going to the bank,' said Curtis. 'We're going to see some friends of mine. They're going to help us. They can make people famous – I mean really famous.'

'What, more famous than Dave and the Sweethearts?' asked C.C.

'Oh yes,' said Curtis. 'Much more famous.'

♫ ♫ ♫

The meeting was in an old, empty building. There was only a long table in the room. A fat, white man sat at the table.

'Who's he?' The man pointed at C.C.

'He's the songwriter.'

'Nice to meet you,' C.C. said nervously.

The man didn't answer. 'Where's the money?' he said to Curtis.

'Here,' said Curtis, and he gave the man the bag of money.

'I leave in three days,' the man said. 'I need all the records by then.'

'That's not a problem,' Curtis said. 'Which radio stations are you taking them to?'

'Don't ask too many questions,' said the man.

Curtis was quiet.

The man was Nicky Cassaro. C.C. didn't know it yet, but Nicky Cassaro was in the Mafia*.

♫ ♫ ♫

'Why did we have to pay Nicky so much money to take our records to the radio stations?' asked C.C.

'Everyone pays,' Curtis told C.C. 'You have to pay if you want your music to get into the right hands.'

C.C. believed him.

'And now we've got three days to record *Steppin' to the Bad Side* and make the records,' said Curtis.

'But that isn't long enough!' said C.C.

'It has to be long enough,' said Curtis.

♫ ♫ ♫

They worked day and night for three days. They recorded the song and made the records. They took the records to Nicky Cassaro.

On radio stations all over the country, DJs played their song.

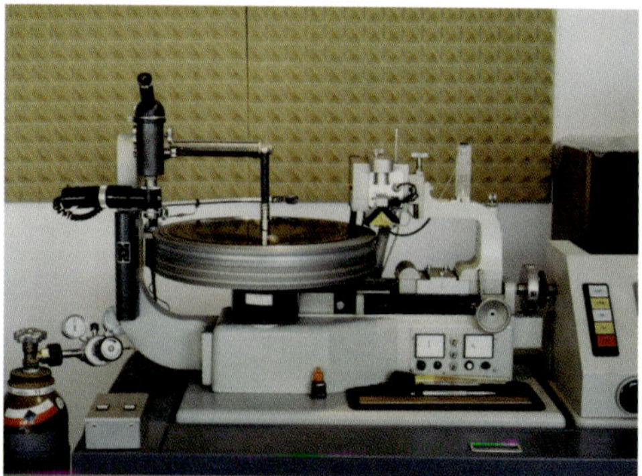

A press for making records.

**The Mafia is an international criminal group.*

CHAPTER 4
The sound of tomorrow

A month later, Curtis ran into Rainbow Records. He had *Billboard* magazine in his hand.

'Number fifteen!' he shouted.

C.C. looked at the magazine. He couldn't believe it, but there it was. *Steppin' to the Bad Side* was on the 'Hot 100' list at number fifteen!

'And I've organised a concert for Jimmy and the girls,' said Curtis. 'It's at the Apollo.'

'The Apollo!' said C.C. 'I don't believe it!'

The Apollo was one of the best theatres black people played in. All the great singers had sung there – Billie Holiday, Ella Fitzgerald, Chuck Berry and Ray Charles.

'We've got a week to practise the new songs. The concert's on June 23rd,' said Curtis.

'June 23rd? Oh no,' said C.C. 'I wanted to go to the civil rights march on June 23rd. It's really important. It's for black people. Martin Luther King* is going to be here,' C.C explained. 'I mean, Martin Luther King, here in Detroit – it's going to be part of *history*.'

'Forget about civil rights. If you want to be part of history, write some more hit records. People don't forget a good song,' Curtis said. 'We've got a concert at the Apollo. Now *that's* important.'

C.C. was angry with Curtis. The fight for civil rights was important, but Curtis only thought about money.

♫ ♫ ♫

The show at the Apollo was a big success. Everybody

** Martin Luther King, Jr. (1929-1968) was a leader of the civil rights movement in the USA.*

loved Jimmy and the girls and their new songs.

'I did it,' Curtis thought, as he watched from the side of the stage. 'Everything's changing now. I know what people like, and I'm going to give it to them. The music business is going to change forever.'

Marty was also watching. He had a feeling he wouldn't be Jimmy's manager for much longer.

♫ ♫ ♫

Effie's life was getting better and better. After the Apollo show, Curtis kissed her. She was in love with him. 'And he's going to help me become a star!' she thought.

Curtis was in his office. He was listening to a recording of Martin Luther King at the Detroit march. Effie came in.

'What are you listening to?' she said.

'Martin Luther King. I recorded him when he spoke at the march,' replied Curtis.

'Don't record him!' said Effie. 'Record me! I'm the star!'

Curtis smiled. 'Hey, baby,' he said, 'why don't you go and find C.C. and practise your new song? I need to find a secretary.' Effie kissed him and left.

♫ ♫ ♫

A lot of people were waiting to see Curtis. Musicians waited outside the studio every day now – they all wanted to record with Rainbow Records.

Curtis held up his hands. The crowd became quiet. 'I promise I'll see all of you. But right now I don't need singers – I need a secretary!'

'I can do it!' a young woman said.

'Are you a secretary?' Curtis asked.

'No, I'm not – I'm a singer! But I can be your secretary, I promise.'

He looked at the girl's excited face. She was very pretty.

'OK,' he said. 'What's your name?'

'Michelle Morris!' she said.

Curtis laughed. 'That sounds great. OK, Michelle, you've got the job!'

♫ ♫ ♫

Marty had been away for a couple of days, so Curtis was organising everything. He was in the showroom, looking at pictures for the new album cover. C.C. was helping him. Curtis's sisters, Rhonda and Janice, were making new dresses for the girls. In one corner, behind a curtain, Deena was trying on her new dress.

'OK,' Curtis said. 'Which picture is best?' Just at that moment, Deena stepped from behind the curtain. She was wearing her new dress. Curtis looked at her. He felt as if he was seeing her for the first time. She looked so beautiful. He couldn't speak.

'What do you think, Curtis?' said Deena. She turned so that Curtis could see her dress better. Curtis didn't say anything.

C.C. didn't notice, but Rhonda and Janice saw. They knew their brother was falling in love.

Just then, Effie walked into the showroom. She was singing a new song. 'C.C. wrote it for me,' she explained. She kissed Curtis.

'What do you think, baby?' she asked. 'It's great, isn't it?'

Curtis stood back from her. 'It's OK,' said Curtis, 'but it's too light.'

'Oh … ' Effie said, 'OK. But when it's right, can I sing it in the concert? You promised I wouldn't spend my life singing back-up, Curtis. I want to be a star!'

'And you will be.' Curtis couldn't look at Effie. He looked at Deena. Her eyes met his, then she looked away.

Effie didn't notice anything. 'Can we talk about it tonight?' Effie asked.

'Sure. Tonight,' Curtis said. He left the room quickly.

♫ ♫ ♫

Marty was back.

'I've only been away a week and you've changed all my plans!' Marty shouted at Curtis. 'You said no to all the theatres on Jimmy's next tour. It took me six months to organise that tour. Six months!'

'Jimmy's too big for those small theatres now. I can get him a show at the Paradise in Miami Beach,' said Curtis, calmly.

'Miami?' Marty laughed. 'You're dreaming! That place is for white people only! Black people can't even park their *cars* there!'

'I've already got him a show there,' Curtis said.

Marty couldn't believe it.

'And Miami's just the beginning! Jimmy could play the Copa, the Americana, even *American Bandstand*'s show,' Curtis continued. 'Jimmy's in the pop charts now. He's hot. We can do this for him.'

'We? *We*'re doing nothing. Jimmy's mine!' Marty shouted.

They hadn't noticed that Jimmy had walked into the office.

'I don't belong to anyone,' Jimmy said quietly.

'Are you agreeing with this … this … car salesman?' Marty said angrily to Jimmy. 'I found you when you were ten years old. I've been your manager since then!'

'Yeah, well, Marty,' Jimmy explained, 'it's a different time now.'

Marty turned to Curtis. 'Do you want him, brother? You've got him. I'm leaving.'

'Hey, wait – ' Jimmy called. 'Marty, I don't want you to go!'

'You can't have it all,' Marty said, and he left.

'Come on, Jimmy. We've got work to do,' said Curtis. But they both watched as Marty drove away. Jimmy felt very sad. Life would never be the same again, without Marty.

CHAPTER 5
A night at the Apollo

It was Lorrell's birthday.

'*Happy birthday to you,*' Jimmy, Effie and Deena sang as Lorrell looked at the beautiful cake Jimmy had bought for her.

'Did you make a wish?' Jimmy asked.

'Oh yes,' Lorrell smiled at him. He gave her a small box

'What's this?' she asked.

'Open it, girl!' said Jimmy.

Lorrell opened the box. She couldn't believe her eyes. Inside was a beautiful ring! She kissed Jimmy. She knew he was married, but she loved him.

'You're mine, baby,' Jimmy said. 'And I'm all yours. It's me and you now.'

Lorrell smiled.

♫ ♫ ♫

The manager of the Paradise Club was speaking to Curtis. 'Tell Jimmy and the others that they can use the dressing room. But they can't go in the dining rooms or the bathrooms.'

'Why?' asked Curtis.

'Darkies* aren't allowed there,' said the manager.

Curtis knew all about racism – he'd grown up with it. But when people used words like 'darkies', it hurt.

'No problem,' Curtis replied. He knew he couldn't let this racism stop them. 'It will be worth it to get an audition for *American Bandstand*,' he thought.

He left the manager's office and went to find the band. They were getting ready.

'Excuse me.' It was one of the waiters. He was black. All the waiters and waitresses were black. 'We'll get you anything you need,' said the waiter. 'Not many black people do shows here. We're all proud of you. Really proud.'

'Thank you,' Jimmy said.

'OK, everyone. Get ready. This is it!' Curtis said. 'I'm going to sit with the producer from *American Bandstand*. We've got to show him that we're really good! Come on, C.C. I want you to meet this guy.'

Curtis found the producer. He was a young white guy.

'Hello,' said Curtis. 'This is C.C., the song-writer.' The producer shook C.C.'s hand. They sat down. Although he looked calm, Curtis was really nervous. 'The show has to be perfect,' he thought. 'Nothing can go wrong tonight. Nothing.'

♫ ♫ ♫

'Please welcome the very talented Jimmy Early and the Dreamettes!' the presenter shouted.

The band played *I Want You Baby*. Curtis and C.C.

* *'Darkies' was a racist word for black people.*

had changed the song to be more attractive to white people. It was much lighter and sweeter. It sounded very romantic. Curtis looked around the room. People seemed to be enjoying the song. Even the producer seemed to be enjoying it.

But Jimmy had a problem with the song. It wasn't his style. He tried to sing it the way Curtis wanted, but he couldn't. So suddenly he started singing in his usual way – loud and sexy. The crowd was shocked. Jimmy didn't care. He danced sexily across the stage. Some people got up and left. Curtis couldn't believe it. What was Jimmy doing? The producer shook his head. He had obviously decided that Jimmy wasn't right for *American Bandstand*.

Curtis looked unhappily round the room. Then he realised that lots of people were looking at Deena. She looked beautiful. Maybe Deena could sing lead? Maybe white people would want to watch her? Curtis had an idea.

♫ ♫ ♫

After the show, Curtis found the the manager of the Paradise Club.

'So, I know there were a few problems with the show. But it was still good, I think,' Curtis said.

'You think so?' the manager asked. 'People here didn't like what Jimmy was doing. All that dancing ... it was too much. I lost money when those people left tonight. The only good thing in your band is that beautiful girl.'

'Deena?' said Curtis. Suddenly, Curtis knew his idea would work. Deena was pretty. White people liked her. Her voice wasn't as strong as Effie's, but it was perfect for the radio. Perfect for pop music.

Curtis knew what he had to do to save Rainbow Records and achieve his dreams. He just had to sell the idea to the girls. The most difficult person was Effie.

Curtis went to find C.C. He knew that if he could persuade C.C., he would be able to persuade Effie.

♫ ♫ ♫

Curtis and C.C. went to the girls' dressing room.

'So, Curtis, did the producer like us?' Deena asked.

'Yes, he liked you. But he didn't like Jimmy. So I'm breaking you and Jimmy up. You're going to open your own act.'

The three girls looked at him in surprise.

'Did you say our *own* act?' Deena asked. 'Just us? No lead singer?'

'*I'm* going to be the lead singer!' Effie cried. 'This is what I've been waiting for. Curtis, I love you!'

'You'll be called the Dreams,' Curtis continued. 'Your first show is next week at the Crystal. There's a lot to do before then. We need to practise the new dances and songs.'

The girls laughed excitedly. They couldn't believe it was true.

Curtis looked at Effie. 'And, Effie – Deena's going to sing lead.'

'Deena's going to do *what*?!' Effie cried. 'Are you joking? She can't sing!' Effie looked at Curtis. 'I always sing lead. Tell him, C.C.'

'We're trying something new, Effie,' said C.C., quietly. He felt very bad.

'You knew about this?' Effie was hurt.

'Curtis and I have just talked about it,' C.C. said. 'He says it's just for now. You can sing lead again later.'

'This is a new sound, with a new look. For kids,' Curtis said. 'And kids watch TV.'

'So, Deena's going to sing lead because she's beautiful?' Effie said quietly. 'Am I ugly, Curtis?' She was crying now.

'Of course not, baby. You know how I feel about you,' Curtis said.

'Effie,' C.C. said, 'your voice alone is too special. We need a lighter sound to get into the pop charts. Later, you can sing lead. But right now, we need Deena's voice.'

'What about what *I* need?' replied Effie, sadly. But she knew that if her biggest fan – her brother – agreed with Curtis, she had no choice. She had to let Deena sing lead. She had to forget her own dreams. For now.

CHAPTER 6
The star of the show

It was the Dreams' first concert. Curtis had invited Deena's mother, May, to the show.

'I'm amazed, Mr Taylor,' May said. 'I never thought my daughter had a great voice.' May couldn't believe it. Her daughter looked amazing and the audience loved her.

'Deena's got something better – she's got something people want,' Curtis said.

'You make her sound like a product,' May said.

Curtis smiled. 'A product. I like that.' He watched Deena on stage and studied the audience. And he knew that he could sell this product. He knew Deena could be a big star.

♫ ♫ ♫

From that day on, Curtis worked on Deena. She had beautiful dresses. She had people to make her hair and face perfect. She had people to give her advice about how to act on stage and how to talk to reporters. And Deena loved it all. Effie tried not to be sad, but she was inside.

♫ ♫ ♫

Six weeks after their first concert, the Dreams' single *Dreamgirls* hit number one on the pop charts. Curtis had invited the press to Rainbow Records to photograph the Dreams as Deena accepted their first gold record*.

* *A 'gold record' is a record that has sold a million copies.*

Deena walked into Curtis's office. 'Curtis, baby, this dress just isn't right. I can't wear it on such an important day!' She didn't notice Effie. Curtis had just refused again to let Effie sing lead and Effie wasn't happy. And now she couldn't believe Deena was talking to *her* boyfriend like this. Why had she called him 'baby'?

'You chose the dress,' Effie said. 'Now you wear it.'

'I didn't ask for *your* opinion,' Deena replied.

Curtis walked over to Deena. 'You look beautiful. Now go and wait for your fans. Today will be wonderful, baby.'

Effie couldn't believe it. What was happening? Did Curtis love Deena? Effie ran out of the room. She expected Curtis to run after her, but he didn't.

Effie didn't want to go to the press meeting for the gold record, but Lorrell persuaded her. Effie didn't enjoy the meeting. The reporters only wanted to talk to Deena. Deena was the star of the show.

♫ ♫ ♫

Things between Effie and Curtis weren't going well. He spent a lot of time away from home. And when he was home, he was too busy to talk to her. Effie was hurt.

One night, Effie was sitting in the kitchen. She was alone and she was feeling sad. Curtis had gone to bed. Suddenly, C.C. ran in. He looked frightened.

'Effie, there's a riot on Twelfth Street!' he cried.

'What?'

'The police arrested some black people,' C.C. explained. 'Then someone threw some bottles at the police, and that started it. They're rioting now.'

'Why are they doing that?' asked Effie, worriedly. 'I don't like it.'

'They're fighting for us, Effie – for our rights,' C.C. said. 'Black people still aren't really free. We don't have the same rights as white people. It isn't fair.'

♫ ♫ ♫

When Effie went to bed that night, Curtis was already asleep. She looked at him. Did he love her, or did he love Deena?

'*This* isn't fair,' she thought, and the tears fell down her face.

♫ ♫ ♫

The next day, C.C. decided to speak to Curtis.

'We could sing about fighting for our rights,' C.C. said to Curtis. 'I've got an idea for a really great song.'

'What are you talking about?' Curtis asked.

'I think we need to fight for our rights,' C.C. explained. 'Don't you?'

'Yes,' Curtis said, 'but music is music. Our songs can't be political. People don't want to hear that sort of song. We're making pop music.'

C.C. didn't agree, but he didn't say anything.

♫ ♫ ♫

They were recording their new single *Heavy, Heavy* when it happened.

'Stop!' said Curtis angrily. 'Effie, you're too loud again.'

'I'm trying to sing quietly, Curtis, but it isn't very easy,' said Effie.

'Well try harder!' he shouted.

Effie felt close to tears. Why was Curtis so angry with her?

They tried again, but Effie's voice was still too strong.

'STOP!' shouted Curtis. He was really angry now. 'Deena's the star, but all we can hear is Effie!' he said.

Effie didn't say anything. She looked upset.

'Maybe we should come back in the morning,' Deena said.

Curtis's voice changed when he spoke to Deena. 'Look, baby, I know you're tired, but let's try one last time. Can we?'

Deena smiled at him.

It was then that Effie knew. 'Curtis is cheating on me. With Deena!' She felt so angry she didn't know what to do.

'Let's do it again,' Curtis said.

When the girls started singing, Effie sang as loud as she could. She shouted. She wanted to show Curtis how angry she was. Deena and Lorrell stopped singing. But Effie didn't stop until the end of the song. Then she ran out of the room.

'Where are you going?' Curtis shouted.

'Curtis, you're cheating on me. And everyone knows it!' Effie screamed.

♫ ♫ ♫

Deena, Lorrell and Effie walked onto the stage of the television programme, *Star Cavalcade*. Deena was nervous about performing on TV. What if something went wrong? Then the music started. Deena sang into the camera.

Effie wanted to sing into the camera, too. But all the cameras were on Deena. She wanted to cry. She felt very angry – angry with Curtis, with Deena, with the world.

'It's always Deena, Deena, Deena!' she thought, and then she knew what to do – she ran off the stage. The other girls didn't know what to do. They tried to keep singing, but they couldn't. They ran off stage after Effie.

'Are you crazy, Effie?' Lorrell asked. 'Why did you do that? We all looked stupid, on television!'

'What's wrong?' Deena asked, although she knew what the problem was.

'You stole my dream, Deena! And you stole my man!' Effie shouted.

'Effie, stop it!' shouted Curtis.

'Why? You don't need me,' Effie shouted. 'You only care about *her*!' She ran outside. In the street outside, Effie was sick. It had happened a few times recently. She decided to go to the doctor.

♫ ♫ ♫

The next big concert was in Las Vegas. Effie didn't come to the practice with the others. Nobody knew where she was.

Just as Lorrell and Deena were singing the last song, Effie finally arrived.

'I'm sorry I'm late!' said Effie. 'I had to go to the doctor's, but I'm feeling better now.'

'Effie … ' C.C. said slowly. 'You … you don't have to do the show tonight.'

'What are you talking about?' Effie laughed.

'Curtis will be back soon. Why don't you rest in your room?' C.C. continued. He sounded nervous.

'I'm fine.' Effie stopped. She looked at Deena and Lorrell. She knew something was wrong.

Then, Michelle Morris, Curtis's secretary, walked onto the stage. She was wearing Effie's dress.

'I'm so nervous. I know the dances, but – ' Michelle stopped when she saw Effie.

'What's going on?' Effie said. Then she realised. She was out of the group!

Just then, Curtis arrived.

'Effie, I was looking for you. I – ' Curtis stopped when he saw Michelle.

'I miss one practice and now I'm out of the group?' Effie said angrily.

'Effie, this isn't just about today,' Curtis replied. 'You're often late and you make trouble all the time. You need a break.'

'A break? You're just saying that because you're cheating on me with *her*.' Effie pointed at Deena.

Curtis looked at Effie. 'You've been trouble, right from the start.'

'Trouble? Curtis, I'm your woman!' Effie cried putting her arms around him.

'But you're destroying this group. I've had enough of you. I'll pay you to leave the group,' Curtis said.

'What?!' cried Effie. 'C.C., did you hear what he said?'

C.C. looked unhappy. 'Effie, I think it's best if you just take the money and go. I'm sorry.'

Effie looked at her brother. 'I don't believe this. Are you my brother?'

'Please, Effie. This time you've gone too far,' C.C. said.

'OK, ' said Curtis, 'everyone just go. I want to talk to Effie. Alone.'

Everyone left. Effie looked at Curtis. He couldn't look at her.

'Effie, there's a show tonight. You'd disappeared. I didn't know where you were. I had to do something.'

Effie didn't say anything.

'Maybe later, you can sing in the group again,' Curtis continued.

Effie just closed her eyes and started singing. When she finished the song, she opened her eyes. She was alone – Curtis had gone.

CHAPTER 7
Deena and the Dreams

Curtis and Deena were in Paris when he asked her to marry him. It was one quiet moment in their very busy lives. Deena was very tired. She was the star of Deena and the Dreams – now one of the most famous groups in the world. She was always busy.

Over the last few years, Curtis had made Rainbow Records into the best record label in the business. The stars of Rainbow Records were bigger than the stars of any other record label. Curtis was an excellent manager and all his groups were famous, but Deena and the Dreams were the most famous.

After Effie left, Deena and Curtis kept their relationship a secret for years. Curtis thought that was best. Deena agreed with Curtis because she loved him. She did exactly what he said. He chose her clothes. He told her how to sing. He even told her what to say to people. Deena had done everything Curtis said, and now she was a huge star. But it hadn't been easy to hide their relationship. And now, at last, Curtis was asking her to marry him.

'Yes, yes, yes – I'll marry you!' Deena cried happily. 'We can buy a big house and have lots of children –'

'Wait a minute,' Curtis said quietly. 'We're going to get married, but there's still a lot of work to do. The Dreams are world-famous now. We can't have a baby at the moment. We're too busy.'

'But … don't you want a family?' Deena asked.

'Of course, baby. Just not now,' Curtis replied. 'In a few years, we can think about it. You understand, don't you?'

Deena was silent for a moment.

'OK,' she said, quietly. 'Whatever you say.'

'Oh, and we're moving to Los Angeles,' he continued. 'I want to get into the movie business too. I want to see your beautiful face in the cinema.'

Deena was surprised.

Curtis explained. 'Adam Brooks, the Hollywood producer, is going to work for me. He's looking at some movie scripts now. You're going to start working on a film very soon.'

'But what about our wedding?' asked Deena.

Curtis smiled. 'We move to L.A. in a month. You'll have the wedding of your dreams, I promise. It'll be amazing.'

♫ ♫ ♫

The wedding *was* amazing. It was huge. There were four hundred guests, and all the press were there. And Brooks even made a film of the wedding. He thought it would help Deena to get the lead in *Cleo* – a new film about Queen Cleopatra. Curtis thought it was a good idea. He wanted Deena to star in *Cleo*. It was the next part of his plan for her.

Deena watched the film of her wedding. 'It's awful,' she thought. 'Adam Brooks has made me look stupid. I've got to talk to Curtis right now. I don't want to make a film with this man.'

She drove to Curtis's office.

'Curtis is in a meeting,' the secretary said.

'I'll wait for him,' Deena replied.

Wayne, C.C. and Adam Brooks were sitting at a table with Curtis. The meeting wasn't going well.

'We've talked to lots of film companies but they're not interested. None of them want to make *Cleo* with Deena,' Brooks explained. 'They don't believe she can act.'

Curtis looked angry. 'Then Rainbow Records will pay for the movie,' he said. Nobody spoke.

'Let's be careful,' Wayne said finally. 'We need to spend more money on the music business. Our stars need new material, especially Jimmy.'

Curtis thought for a moment. 'OK, let's do a TV programme to celebrate Jimmy's anniversary. We'll get enough money from that to pay for the film.' Then he left the meeting and went to his office.

He kissed Deena. 'How's my favourite wife?'

Deena was nervous. 'Curtis, I'm not sure how to tell you this.'

'Just say it, baby,' Curtis said.

'I know how important *Cleo* is for you, but … I can't play that part,' Deena said finally.

'Of course you can. You're just nervous,' he laughed.

'No, Curtis, you don't understand,' Deena said.

Curtis looked at her. 'I promised to make you a movie star. *Cleo* is an important part. Cleopatra was a queen, she's the star of the film. Black women never get parts like that.'

'Oh, I know, Curtis –'

'And it's more than just you,' he continued. 'Think of all those other beautiful black actresses. One day they're going to say, "I can play any part I want. Look at Deena Jones, she did it."'

'But Cleopatra's *sixteen* years old in the movie,' Deena said. 'It's not the right part for me.'

Curtis kissed her again. 'You'll always be sixteen to me.'

'Maybe that's the problem,' Deena said. 'I'm not a girl any more. I'm a woman. And you won't let me be myself.'

'All I want is to make you happy, baby,' Curtis replied. He put his arms around her.

'You know what I want,' she said. 'Please, Curtis. Let's have a child.'

Curtis suddenly dropped his arms. He looked angry. 'I've got another meeting,' he said, and left.

♫ ♫ ♫

'Magic, read your book, please,' Effie said to her daughter. Magic was a slim, pretty seven-year-old. She had her father's eyes, but her personality was like her mother's.

They were in the welfare office. The welfare officer was asking her mother questions. Magic couldn't understand why her mother came here.

Effie did it because she had no choice. After leaving the Dreams, she had tried to become a star on her own. It was hard to get shows and she had to pay the other musicians in the band. By the time Magic was three, Effie had spent all the money Curtis had given her. Then Effie had to sell her house. She was a good mother, but it was hard. Sometimes she drank too much, just to forget.

When they got home, Ronald, Effie's father was there. He gave her a letter. 'It's from your brother. There's money in there.'

'You spend it,' Effie said. She hadn't spoken to C.C. or replied to his letters since she left the group. She hadn't forgiven him.

Ronald shook his head. 'Look, I know you think your brother betrayed you, but it wasn't just him. Maybe what he did was wrong, but you were wrong, too. You made trouble,' he said.

He had said the same thing many times. He was always trying to help her to start again.

'Go home,' Effie said quietly. She waited until he had gone and then she got a drink. But she couldn't stop thinking about her father's words.

Finally, she made a decision. 'Curtis destroyed my career. I need to build it again. I need to build my life again. I'll go and see Marty in the morning. I'll do it – for me, and for Magic.'

CHAPTER 8
'We're through'

C.C. had written a new song for Jimmy. It wasn't just another pop song – this was something different. Black artists like James Brown and Aretha Franklin were using their music to sing about the fight for civil rights. Jimmy and C.C. wanted to do the same.

And now Curtis and Deena were listening to the song for the first time. Jimmy, C.C., Lorrell and Michelle were at their house. Jimmy was very nervous. Would Curtis like the song? Would he let Jimmy sing it?

Jimmy listened to his and Lorrell's voices as they sang *Patience*. When the record finished, there was silence. Everyone waited.

Finally, Curtis spoke. 'It's good, man. It's really good.'

Jimmy smiled. C.C. smiled, too. He was tired of always writing pop songs. He wanted Rainbow Records to make some real records – records that celebrated the fight for civil rights. More and more black artists were doing that, and C.C. wanted to be part of it.

'We wanted to surprise you, Curtis,' he said excitedly.

Deena turned to C.C. 'It's wonderful. I loved it.'

'Yes, it's really good,' Curtis continued. 'But it's a message song. It's got a political message. That's not good.'

'This song tells the truth,' Michelle said.

'That's right,' C.C. added. 'Music should show what people are feeling.'

Curtis stood up. 'No. Music should sell records and make us rich. Jimmy, we'll find some new material for you. Deena, come on, there's a guy I want you to meet.' He walked out.

'Jimmy, I'm so sorry,' Deena said. She put her hand on his arm, then she turned to follow Curtis. Nobody spoke as she left.

Jimmy took something from his pocket.

Lorrell shook her head. 'Jimmy, you don't need drugs. Don't take them.'

But Jimmy needed his drugs now. His music wasn't very popular. He didn't give many concerts any more. He spent a lot of time at home with his wife, Melba. He wasn't enjoying his life. And as he became more unhappy, he took drugs more and more often. And Curtis knew that.

♫ ♫ ♫

'Jimmy, I want to talk to you.' Curtis closed his office door. Jimmy knew it was an important meeting. C.C. had already told him that Curtis was planning a big TV show.

'We're doing a special TV show,' Curtis said.

'Yeah, I heard that,' Jimmy replied. 'I can do an old song. But I want C.C. to write some new songs for me because – '

'Jimmy,' Curtis said. 'I only put you in the show because some people like you. But you've got to stop taking drugs.'

'But – ' Jimmy said.

'I'm serious, Jimmy. If you do this show well, we can see about some new songs for you,' Curtis said. 'But no more drugs.'

'I – ' Jimmy started to speak but Curtis didn't want to hear any more. 'I've got to go. The show's next Tuesday. You're going to be clean. And remember, no sexy dancing. They just want a nice song. OK?'

'Yeah, right. A nice song,' Jimmy said as Curtis left.

♫ ♫ ♫

The producer knocked on Jimmy's dressing room door.

'Mr Early, you're next.'

Inside, Lorrell was giving Jimmy another cup of coffee. 'I thought you had to stay clean tonight,' she said. 'You know how important this TV show is.'

'It's Melba's fault. She said she wanted to come tonight. I said no, but she wouldn't listen. Then she put on her best dress!'

Lorrell stopped. 'Are you telling me that your wife is in the audience? Right now?' she asked.

'What could I do? That's why I needed to relax.' Jimmy said. He didn't notice that Lorrell looked angry.

'You know,' Lorrell said, 'it's our anniversary too, baby. Don't you remember? Let's see … one, two, three, four, five, six, seven, eight. We've been together for eight years.'

The producer knocked again.

'I promise, Lorrell, I'll tell her,' Jimmy said as he left. 'I'll tell her about us, and we'll be together, baby.'

'But when, Jimmy. When?' Lorrell followed him to the side of the stage.

'I just need a little more time. I love you, Lorrell. You know I do,' Jimmy said.

Lorrell looked at the love of her life. She wanted to believe him.

'But right now, I've got a show to do,' Jimmy said.

'No more,' Lorrell thought, as she watched Jimmy run on stage. 'No more.'

Jimmy was on stage singing. Everything was going well, just as Curtis wanted. But suddenly Jimmy stopped singing. 'I can't do it,' he said to the audience. 'I can't sing this sad song. This programme is a celebration … a celebration of Rainbow Records!'

The audience laughed. Curtis looked very angry.

'What's he doing?' the director asked.

But Jimmy and the band had started to play a different song. It wasn't 'nice' – it was sexy. The audience went wild. Jimmy took off his jacket. He moved just like in the old days. Then he took off his tie. Curtis ran to the side of the stage. 'Lorrell, did you know about this?' he asked her.

'Curtis,' Lorrell said, 'I'm just as surprised as you.'

'*Jimmy's the man*,' Jimmy sang. The audience loved it. When Jimmy left the stage, they shouted for more.

'Hey, Curtis,' Jimmy laughed. 'Did you like my show?'

'You looked stupid!' Curtis said angrily.

'No – I was just being Jimmy,' Jimmy said.

'Curtis, Jimmy keeps asking you for something new. But you just don't listen,' Lorrell said.

'We're through,' Curtis said. 'I'm sorry, Jimmy. It's over.'

'What do you mean it's over? You can't do this to me!' Jimmy shouted.

Curtis held out his hand. 'Come on, let's try to finish as friends,' he said. But Jimmy didn't shake his hand.

Lorrell walked towards the stage. The Dreams were ready to sing next.

Jimmy caught her arm. 'Wait a minute, baby. I need you now. I love you.'

Lorrell kissed him. 'I love you, too. But we're through. I've got a show to do. Remember? I've got a show to do.'

'And now, please welcome Rainbow's biggest star! Deena Jones with the Dreams!' the presenter cried.

Jimmy watched. Then, slowly, he turned to leave. 'I was here before you and I'll be here after you!' he shouted. But nobody was listening.

CHAPTER 9
Good news, bad news

Hollywood, Los Angeles. Deena was sitting at a table by a hotel swimming pool, trying to change her life. She was talking to Jerry Harris, a film producer, and Sam Walsh, a director. They were talking about their new movie. Deena wanted to be in the film. She hadn't told Curtis, though. Curtis still wanted her to be in *Cleo*.

'The problem is, you're too beautiful,' Harris said. 'This movie's about three people who have lost everything. They have just one last chance. Dawn doesn't look beautiful. She's fighting for her life.'

Deena smiled. 'But that's what I love about her,' she said. 'Of course, the script needs some work.'

Walsh didn't look happy. 'What do you mean?' he asked. 'I spent a year on this script.'

'And it's good,' Deena replied. 'But she's not real yet. What about her name, for example? I've never met a black woman called Dawn.'

'Let's get together and look at the script,' Walsh suggested.

'I'd like that,' Deena smiled.

'I hear Curtis still wants to make that crazy film, *Cleo*,' Harris said.

'Curtis is busy with the music business right now,' Deena said. 'That's why I didn't want to worry him about our meeting today.'

Everyone knew it was a lie, but, in true Hollywood style, they said nothing.

'But will Curtis let you do this film?' Harris asked.

'That won't be a problem, Jerry,' Deena said. This was exactly why she needed to make her own plans. Her contract with Rainbow Records said that Curtis could make decisions about nearly everything – he almost owned Deena. But Deena didn't want Curtis to make all the decisions for her now. She wanted to take control of her own life.

♫ ♫ ♫

'I didn't think it was possible, Curtis!' C.C. shouted angrily. 'I didn't think you could take even more heart out of my music.'

'I just made it easier to dance to,' Curtis said calmly.

'What about the words? You've taken all the feeling out of the song!' C.C. said.

'This is a new sound, totally new, bigger than rock, or anything else. People want to dance again – and when they dance, they'll be dancing to our music!' Curtis said.

'*Your* music, Curtis. This isn't *my* music,' C.C. said angrily.

'Come on, C.C.,' Curtis said. C.C. was about to leave when Curtis's sisters Rhonda and Janice appeared. They were crying.

'Now what's going on?' Curtis asked.

Then Lorrell ran into the room. She was screaming. Deena and Michelle came in after her. Deena tried to hold Lorrell, but she couldn't.

Michelle told them the terrible news. 'Jimmy Early's dead.'

♫ ♫ ♫

Lorrell was sitting on a sofa in Deena's house. She was quiet now. Deena had her arms round her while they all watched the news on TV. Jimmy had taken too many drugs and died.

'It's terrible,' Curtis said. Lorrell looked at him, but

didn't say anything.

C.C. got up to leave. 'I'm going now,' he said. He didn't look at Curtis.

'C.C., nothing is more important than family. I know we've had problems, but we're still family,' Curtis said.

'It's over, Curtis,' C.C. said. He'd waited all day to say those words. Now he could go.

'Jimmy killed himself,' Curtis shouted. 'You know that. I didn't kill him! I didn't!'

C.C. didn't answer. He left the house, got in his car and drove to the airport. He took the first plane to Detroit.

When he arrived, he just drove around the city, thinking.

'How did it all end like this?' he wondered. 'Effie had to leave. Jimmy's dead. Curtis … Curtis only thinks about the business. He doesn't care about people.'

C.C. thought about Effie. He needed to find her. He wanted her to forgive him.

♫ ♫ ♫

C.C. had been in Effie's flat for two hours. He was with his dad, waiting for Effie. He couldn't believe how awful the place was.

'But Dad, I sent her money,' he said. 'I sent her enough money to live better than this.'

'She wouldn't spend your money,' Ronald explained. He showed C.C. a box. It contained all of C.C.'s letters – many of them were unopened. They were all full of money.

C.C. looked round the flat again.

'Effie must sleep here on the sofa,' he thought. 'There's only one bedroom. It's got toys in it. A child's room.'

Suddenly, they heard voices on the stairs.

'Mama, why do you walk so slowly?' a girl's voice said.

'Because I'm old, baby.' It was Effie.

C.C. ran to the door. Magic opened it and looked surprised.

'Who are you?' she asked.

'This is your uncle,' Ronald said to Magic.

But when Effie saw C.C. she turned and ran back down the stairs. C.C. followed.

'Effie!' he cried, but she didn't stop. She ran outside and hid behind a tree. She waited until C.C. had gone away.

Effie had been angry with C.C. for a very long time. She'd missed him, too, but she didn't know how to suddenly stop being angry.

'How can I just forgive him?' she thought.

♫ ♫ ♫

'Goodnight, Dad,' C.C. said unhappily.

'Don't worry, C.C.,' Ronald said. 'It'll be OK. Effie needs you now more than ever. Find her. Help her to understand that she can be a great singer again.'

♫ ♫ ♫

When Effie finally went back to the flat, her father was waiting for her.

'At least listen to C.C.,' he said. 'He's not working with Curtis any more, Effie. He wants to help you to get a recording contract.'

'I don't need him,' Effie said angrily. 'He betrayed me! He let Curtis throw me out of the group!'

'Did you expect your brother to forget his own dreams, Effie?' Ronald said. 'He had to stay there. Aren't you happy that he's a famous song-writer now? It was his one chance. And he tried to help you. He always wrote to you and sent you money. Curtis threw you out of the group. C.C. couldn't stop him. Don't be angry with C.C., Effie.

Don't be selfish.'

Effie knew her father was right. 'But C.C. *was* wrong,' she thought.

CHAPTER 10
One Night Only

The next night, C.C. went to Effie's favourite club. He thought there was a chance Effie would be there – and he was right. There she was on stage singing with her amazing voice. She finished her song and went over to talk to Marty, Jimmy's old manager! C.C. didn't know this, but Marty had agreed to be Effie's manager now.

C.C. wanted to talk to his sister, but he didn't know what to say. He sat at the bar and watched her. Then suddenly Effie got up and walked towards the bar. When she saw C.C., she stopped.

'What are you doing here?' she asked. 'You left town a long time ago.'

'Effie,' he said, 'please –'

'Why did you come here, after all these years?' she said angrily.

'Effie, there's nothing I can say … except I was young and I made a mistake.'

Effie looked at him.

'I promised I'd write you a hit song, Effie. Let me do it

for you now,' he continued.

'I don't need you!' Effie cried.

'No, Effie – *I* need *you*.' C.C. tried to put his arm around his sister, but she pulled away from him. 'I'm sorry, Effie,' he said.

'Sorry? You betrayed me!' Effie still looked angry.

'Effie, I can't change the past, but I have a song now – a real song. And I think only you can sing it right. Let me help you. Let's do what we always wanted to do – together.'

Effie didn't speak for a long time. 'I've waited so long to hear that,' she said finally.

'Effie, sing my song the way it should be,' C.C. said. He put his arm round his sister, and this time she didn't move away.

♫ ♫ ♫

Effie recorded the song a few days later. As C.C. listened to Effie singing his song, he felt happy at last. 'This is how things should be,' he thought. 'Effie's the only person to sing my songs. This is the start of something real.'

♫ ♫ ♫

Magic sat next to the radio. She was so proud – her mother was singing on the radio! As they listened, Effie, C.C. and Ronald felt proud, too.

'And that was Effie White with her new song *One Night Only*,' the DJ said.

That night, as she celebrated in her tiny flat with her family around her, Effie felt she was the happiest person in the world.

♫ ♫ ♫

In Los Angeles, Curtis was listening to Effie's new song too. He was worried. Effie was too good.

'The record's only being played on local black radio stations around Detroit,' Wayne said, 'but it's becoming successful.'

'If C.C. wrote it, then *I* own it,' Curtis said angrily.

'I guess so,' said Wayne. 'He still has a contract with Rainbow Records. Our lawyers can ask for half the money Effie and C.C. make from the record.'

'No. This is the perfect song for our new sound. I want to record it with Deena and the girls.'

Wayne knew Curtis did some awful things – but this? Even Wayne was surprised. 'Come on, Curtis,' he said. 'This is Effie's big break. There are other songs.'

'This is business, Wayne. Now organise it,' Curtis said coldly.

♫ ♫ ♫

Curtis's producers took *One Night Only* and changed it. It was a serious song, but they made it fast and light, for dancing. The new sound was 'disco'. Deena and the others didn't recognise the song when they recorded it. They hadn't heard Effie on the radio. They didn't know she was becoming successful with *One Night Only*.

A week later, Deena and the Dreams had another hit record – *One Night Only*. It was playing on the radio all over the country.

Then they did a show at the New York Dance Club. As Curtis watched, he knew that Rainbow's new sound was a success. Disco music had been born – it would be big business. The record was a huge hit.

And then Johnny Carson asked Deena and the Dreams to appear on *The Tonight Show*. The girls were delighted. Millions of people watched the show. They were *really* famous now.

♫ ♫ ♫

Effie, C.C., Marty and Magic were watching *The Tonight Show* when they saw Deena and the Dreams on it. They couldn't believe it. The Dreams had stolen Effie's song!

Johnny Carson asked Deena where the song was from. Deena didn't know. 'Did you know this song is Effie's?' he asked. Deena looked shocked. She didn't know what to say.

The Tonight Show with Johnny Carson

Johnny Carson asked the girls to sing the song on TV. When Magic heard it, she started crying. She ran to her room and lay on her bed. 'Mom will never be a success now,' she thought. 'It isn't fair. Why does everybody always steal things from her?'

'I'm so sorry, Effie,' C.C. said.

'It's not your fault, little brother. It's Curtis,' Effie said. 'Now everyone will know what Curtis is really like,' she thought.

♫ ♫ ♫

Deena was in the dressing room at the NBC television studios. She had just finished the interview with Johnny Carson. She was angry.

'Why didn't anybody tell me about Effie's song?' she asked. Nobody answered.

'The way Johnny Carson talked about it, it sounded like we *stole* the song!'

'That's what we did, isn't it?' Lorrell said quietly.

'What?' Deena cried.

'Come on, Deena … Effie's song was on the radio. We took the song and recorded it. Then our record became more successful than hers.'

Deena got her coat. 'I'm ready to go. Now!'

CHAPTER 11
The plan

Curtis was talking about *Cleo* again, but Deena wasn't really listening. She was thinking about her last secret meeting with Harris and Walsh. She had finally signed the contract for their new film. She was playing the lead! Deena knew Curtis would be angry when she told him, but she didn't care. She was angry with him about Effie's song.

Curtis was still crazy about getting into movies. He was hoping that his new disco hits would pay for his first film, *Cleo*. He was sure the film would be a success. Then he would be the biggest manager in Los Angeles – music *and* movies! That was his plan.

Deena knew all about Curtis's plan – he hadn't told her, but she knew. A few days ago, when Curtis wasn't there, she'd gone into his office. She'd looked at all his papers. She was tired of never knowing Curtis's plans for her future. She wanted information. And she knew she would find it in her husband's office. She found a lot of old papers – papers from the start of Rainbow Records. Some of the papers were *very* interesting …

♫ ♫ ♫

Curtis was still talking about *Cleo*. 'So, it's finally going to happen!' he said.

'Oh, OK, baby,' Deena said. 'How can I tell him that I've signed a different film contract?' she thought.

'What's wrong?' Curtis asked.

'Maybe I'm just tired,' Deena said.

'Yeah, it's been a crazy time,' Curtis said. 'Interviews,

concerts … And all your secret meetings.'

'How did Curtis know about those?' she thought.

'When were you going to tell me?' Curtis asked coldly.

'I'm sorry … I wanted to tell you, but … It's just … it's such a great part. And it's exactly the kind of movie I want to make.'

Curtis was silent.

'Curtis,' Deena continued, 'the music business is in your blood. But movies are different.'

'Deena, do you know why I chose you to sing lead? Your voice has no personality … nothing but what *I* put in it,' Curtis said. 'I only chose you to sing lead because you look good. People like to watch you. They don't care about your voice. You aren't a singer – you're my product.'

He wanted to hurt her. He succeeded.

'They offered me the part and I'm taking it,' she replied.

'Oh, yeah? Read your contract. You can't do anything unless I agree,' Curtis said quietly.

'I'll get a lawyer,' Deena said. 'I don't care how long it takes. I'm going to be free, Curtis.'

'Do you think Harris and Walsh will wait for you?' Curtis laughed. 'Don't be stupid. They'll find another actress. And I'm sorry, but I won't let you do that part.'

Curtis left. Deena felt like her world was ending. Would she ever be free, really? But then suddenly she knew what she had to do.

♫ ♫ ♫

A little later that day, Deena put some of Curtis's papers into a big envelope. Her hand was shaking as she wrote Effie's address. Then, she posted the envelope.

♫ ♫ ♫

Effie opened the envelope and read the letter. 'Dear Effie, this is your chance to be a star. Deena,' was all it said.

Effie looked at the papers. They included lists of DJs' names, radio stations and payments of money. At the top of one paper someone had written, 'Curtis, I've been to these stations. Tell C.C. to bring more records and I'll go to the other stations, Nicky.'

'C.C., your name is on here,' Effie said. 'What is this? Who's Nicky?'

C.C. looked at all the papers and then he laughed.

'Nicky Cassaro. It's a list of all the DJs that Curtis paid to play Rainbow Records' songs. He paid DJs to push Rainbow Records up the Top 100. That's bribery! We can use this against Curtis!' He kissed his sister.

♫ ♫ ♫

The next day, Effie, C.C. and Marty talked to a lawyer, David Bennett.

'This could destroy Rainbow Records,' Bennett explained. 'Bribing DJs to play records is against the law.'

'What about C.C.?' Marty asked. 'His name is on those papers too.'

'You could go to prison,' Bennett explained to C.C.

Effie wanted to forget the whole thing. 'Curtis has done enough to this family. I don't want to lose you again, C.C.'

'No, Effie,' C.C. said. 'I believed Curtis when he told me that paying DJs was normal. I didn't protect you when Curtis made you leave the group. If I have to go to prison, then I'll go. But Curtis must pay for what he's done.'

'Curtis doesn't want to go to prison. He'll do anything to save himself,' Marty said. 'Leave it to me.'

Marty talked to Bennett and together they made a plan.

♫ ♫ ♫

Deena was recording a new song, *I'm Moving On*. As she sang, she thought about what she'd done.

'I've betrayed Curtis,' she thought. 'He loved me and he made me a star. But now I have to live my own life.'

Curtis was listening. He could hear the feeling in Deena's voice.

Wayne arrived. 'C.C. and Marty are here with a white man. They want to see you, Curtis.'

'Tell them to go away,' Curtis replied.

'You have to talk to them. They say they've got some papers … with Nicky Cassaro's name on them,' Wayne said nervously.

♫ ♫ ♫

C.C., Marty and David Bennett were in the meeting room. Curtis sat down.

'Mr Taylor, we're going to go to the police,' Bennett said.

'Who is this guy?' Curtis said angrily to C.C. and Marty.

'Our lawyer,' C.C. said.

Bennett put copies of Curtis's papers on the table. 'These papers show that you bribed DJs to play your records. Nicky Cassaro is in the Mafia. You paid the Mafia.'

'You're going to prison,' C.C. said.

'Who gave you these papers? They're from my office at home!' Suddenly Curtis stopped. He realised that Deena had betrayed him. He couldn't believe it. His Deena? How could she do this to him?

♫ ♫ ♫

Effie was in the studio with Deena. After Deena had sent the papers, the two women had arranged to meet.

'Effie … I've wanted to see you so many times,' she said. 'How are you?'

'I'm happy now, Deena,' Effie replied. 'I have a child who loves me.'

Deena was surprised. 'You have a baby?'

'Well, Magic is almost nine now,' Effie explained.

'Magic must be Curtis's child!' Deena realised. 'Curtis always refused to have a child with me, but Effie had his baby.' It hurt.

Just then, Curtis walked into the room.

'Deena, he doesn't know about Magic,' Effie said quickly and left the room.

'I'll talk to you later,' Curtis said angrily to his wife. He followed Effie.

C.C., Marty and Bennett were waiting for her in the hall. 'So?' she asked.

'Mr Taylor has agreed to our plan,' Bennett said. 'He doesn't want to go to prison.'

C.C. smiled. 'He's agreed to send *your* record to shops

and radio stations all over the country.'

'And we'll have our own label,' Marty added.

'And he's going to pay for everything!' Bennett finished.

Effie laughed. 'Sounds good to me.'

Curtis appeared. He wanted to talk to Effie, but she walked straight past him.

'Just remember, Curtis. If you don't do everything we've agreed, you'll go to prison,' C.C. said.

'That's right, Curtis. You stopped me once, but you're never going to stop me again,' Effie said. She turned and walked out of the door. C.C., Marty and Bennett followed her.

Curtis walked angrily back to the studio. He wanted to talk to Deena. But the room was empty – Deena had gone.

CHAPTER 12
Goodbye, Dreamgirls

Deena didn't love Curtis any more. He wasn't the man she had thought he was. She realised that Curtis didn't really care about people – he didn't know how to love. And for so many years he hadn't let Deena have a child. He hadn't thought about Deena's feelings – just about his plans for being rich, successful and famous. Now Deena felt that Curtis had never really loved her.

Deena wanted to be free, and now everything was nearly ready. She had been to a lawyer and he was helping her to leave Rainbow Records. Her mother, May, had also flown in from Detroit to help her daughter. May stayed at a hotel so that Curtis didn't know. Together, Deena and May met the managers from other record companies. They all wanted to give Deena a contract – not to be in a group, but to sing on her own. And now, finally, Deena had to tell Curtis she was leaving.

♫ ♫ ♫

When Curtis got home, there was a taxi outside the house. He ran inside.

'Deena! Where are you?' he shouted angrily.

May walked into the house.

Curtis was surprised. 'May, what are you doing here?'

'Deena needed me, so here I am,' she replied. Just then, Deena came out.

'Please wait in the taxi, Mama,' she said.

Curtis waited until May had gone outside. 'You betrayed me, Deena,' he said. He was very angry. 'You're my wife!'

'I had to do something to stop you,' Deena said. 'How could you do that to Effie? '

'Forget about Effie,' Curtis replied. 'She isn't important. Deena and the Dreams are important. We needed that song, baby.'

Deena picked up her suitcase.

'Where do you think you're going?' Curtis asked.

'I'm leaving,' she said.

Curtis couldn't believe this was really happening. 'Come on, Deena! You can't leave!'

'Why?' she shouted. 'Because you own me? You can take everything I have, Curtis. It doesn't matter. I'll start again. Effie did it, and so can I.'

'I love you, baby. You're my dream,' he said.

Deena looked at him. 'But now I've got dreams of my own. And I can't let you take those dreams from me. And I can't stay here any more. I'm sorry, Curtis. Goodbye.' She went out to the taxi.

'To the airport, please,' she said to the driver.

Deena and her mother were flying back home to Detroit.

♫ ♫ ♫

Curtis watched as they drove away. There was nothing he could do. He realised that his life was empty without Deena. And what about Rainbow Records? He put his head in his hands. What would he do next?

♫ ♫ ♫

'Do you really think that Effie will sing with you again?' May asked.

'I don't know, Mama,' Deena said. 'Maybe she'll say no. But I have to ask her to be part of our last concert. It will be wonderful – the three of us on stage, together again. I hope she'll say yes.'

♫ ♫ ♫

Deena stood outside Effie's flat. She was nervous. She knocked on the door and C.C. opened it. Inside, Lorrell, Michelle and Marty were sitting at the small kitchen table. Effie was on the sofa with Magic.

'Hello,' they all said, except Effie.

'As you probably know, I've left Rainbow Records. You all know why,' Deena explained. 'Curtis did a very bad thing when he stole Effie's record. I don't want to talk to him again. And now I'm going to sing on my own.'

'I knew,' smiled Lorrell. During the last week, Lorrell had thought a lot about her own life. She loved being a star, but she realised that she'd missed a lot of other things. 'I understand,' Lorrell continued. 'And I'm going to stop singing. I'm tired. I want to get married and have kids.'

'So that's it. No more Dreams,' said Effie. 'Good.'

'Effie, it isn't finished yet. We're doing one last concert. I came here to ask you to sing with me again,' Deena said slowly.

Effie couldn't believe it. 'Sing? With you?'

'Please just listen to her, Effie,' C.C. said.

'Look,' Deena said, 'I didn't come here to upset you. It's a business idea. I want us to do a goodbye concert here, at the Detroit Theatre. When we sing *Dreamgirls*, I want you to sing the lead, Effie.'

Effie thought about it.

'Effie, there will be lots of important record producers at the concert. They'll all want to work with you after they hear your voice,' Deena said.

'And Curtis?' Effie asked.

'He has nothing to do with this,' Deena explained. 'That man won't destroy our dreams again. Ever.'

'Come on, Effie,' C.C. said.

'Yeah, come on, Effie,' Lorrell said. 'Let's do it!'

Effie was silent.

♫ ♫ ♫

Lorrell asked the driver to stop outside the theatre. She smiled as she read the sign: DEENA JONES AND THE DREAMS – THE GOODBYE CONCERT.

'Come on,' Deena said. 'Let's go inside.'

An hour later, Curtis arrived. The theatre was full – the audience was already excited.

'Mr Taylor, how does it feel to say goodbye to the Dreams?' a reporter asked.

'They're all talented ladies,' Curtis said. 'I'm happy that they want to explore new possibilities. And I want you to say hello to Tania Williams.' He pointed to a beautiful girl. 'Tania's album will be out next month. It's a totally new sound. It's –'

Just then Effie arrived and her fans started screaming. C.C. and Magic were behind her.

'Miss White,' a reporter called. 'Your record is at number one. You must be excited.'

'It feels good, yes,' Effie said.

The reporter looked at Magic. 'And who's this?' he asked.

Effie looked at Curtis. 'This is Magic, my daughter.'

Curtis realised that Magic was his daughter. For a second, his eyes met Effie's. Then he went inside.

♫ ♫ ♫

'Ladies and gentlemen,' the presenter cried, 'in their goodbye concert – the incredible Deena and the Dreams!'

Everyone in the audience stood up. They were shouting and screaming for the Dreams. Then Deena started to sing. The goodbye concert had begun.

When it was nearly the end of the show, Deena walked to the centre of the stage.

'This is the last song,' she told the audience. 'You know, we've been together for a long time. I promised that I wouldn't cry. And I won't, I'm very happy. But many of you know that there aren't only three Dreams there are four. And tonight we're *all* here to sing our special song for you. Here she is … Effie!'

The audience went wild when Effie walked onto the stage. The music for their song *Dreamgirls* started. As Effie sang lead, she looked at Magic. She knew that her daughter was really proud of her.

She sang.

And it was amazing.

Actors from the Broadway show

In December 1981 the musical *Dreamgirls* opened at the Imperial Theatre on Broadway in New York. It quickly became a huge hit. It was on Broadway for four years – an amazing 1,521 shows! Twenty-five years after audiences first saw the show, *Dreamgirls* finally became a film. How did they make the movie? How did they choose the actors?

A talented writer and director

Bill Condon

Bill Condon was at the opening night of *Dreamgirls* on Broadway. For a long time he wanted to make *Dreamgirls* into a movie. After his success as the writer of the musical film *Chicago*, he was able to make his dream come true.

Shooting the film

Filming of *Dreamgirls* started in January 2006 and took four months. Although the story takes place in Detroit, none of the filming was done there. It was mainly filmed in studios in Los Angeles.

What do these words mean? You can use a dictionary.
musical role finalist nominated / nomination award

Finding the actors

The film producers knew it was very important to find exactly the right people for the biggest roles in *Dreamgirls*. After all, many of them had to be fantastic singers as well as actors.

Beyoncé Knowles

They tried several actresses for the part of Deena, but none of them seemed right. Then they met Beyoncé and she was perfect.

Eddie Murphy

People usually think of Eddie Murphy as a comic actor, but he was fantastic in the serious role of Jimmy Early. He was nominated for an Oscar® for this role.

Jennifer Hudson

783 actresses tried for the part of Effie. Finally, they chose Jennifer Hudson, who was one of the finalists in the hit TV show *American Idol*. Hudson won an Oscar® for the role.

Did you know ...?

Jamie Foxx (Curtis) is a very famous actor, but he's also a very talented singer. His album, *Unpredictable*, was number 1 in the USA. He has received many awards and nominations for both his acting and his singing.

Do you like musical shows and films? If yes, what's your favourite? If not, what kind of films and shows do you like?

Beyoncé Knowles

American singer and actress Beyoncé is very talented. She doesn't just sing, dance and act – she's also a record producer, fashion designer and model! She became famous as the lead singer of Destiny's Child – one of the most successful girl groups ever. Since appearing in *Dreamgirls* she's also a hot film star … What does she think of *Dreamgirls* and being famous?

In *Dreamgirls* you play Deena Jones, a singer who follows her dreams to become a star. Was this a dream part for you?
It's definitely a dream part for me. *Dreamgirls* is all about the ups and downs that come with being famous. It's about friendship and these women and their journeys. In the end, they realise what their true dreams are.

***Dreamgirls* looks back at the history of girl groups. Have you learned any lessons while looking back?**
Yes! You can't satisfy everyone. When I was younger I tried to make sure that everyone was happy. But everyone has different opinions, and that's OK. You have to make sure you are happy with yourself. That's really the most important thing.

Do you prefer singing and dancing to acting?
I was a singer before I even knew I wanted to act. But I do enjoy acting. It's really important to me now that I've done a movie that I love. I wanted to do this movie so much that I dedicated myself 100% to it.

What are the best and the worst parts of being so famous?
The best parts are being able to live my dreams and tour around the world. I've done shows with Prince and many other people I admire. The worst part is that there's always someone looking at everything I do. That's hard sometimes.

On stage with Prince

Would you like to be a singer or an actor / actress? What do you need to be successful?

Have you got any dreams for the future?

Well, my mother and I have a fashion line. My grandmother made clothes for my mother and my mother made clothes for me. She always wanted to be a designer and have a fashion label. It's fantastic to help her dream come true. Also, I hope to be the first African-American woman to win an Oscar® and a Grammy.

So, you want to follow your dreams? Beyoncé says ...

- ☆ It's really important to make sure the people around you are supportive. Don't listen to people who don't believe in you.
- ☆ Be sure about what you want and focus on it. Maybe you'll have to work when your friends are going to parties and staying up late. But if it's what you want, then just do it!

What do these words mean? You can use a dictionary.

model satisfy dedicated admire supportive focus

'I HAVE A DREAM'

***Dreamgirls* takes place in the 1960s and 1970s. These were times of huge political change in the USA.**

Segregation

In the early 1960s, nearly one hundred years after the end of slavery, black people still did not have the same rights as white people. In 1954 the high court in the USA said that racial segregation in schools was against the law. However, there was still segregation on buses and in restaurants, theatres and other public places.

Black people had to ride at the back of buses.

Martin Luther King, Jr.

The Civil Rights Movement

Martin Luther King, Jr. was an important civil rights leader. King believed that non-violent protest was the best way to make changes. He organized marches for black people's rights. In August 1963 he led the March on Washington for Jobs and Freedom. About 250,000 people were on the march. At the end of the march, King made his famous 'I have a dream' speech. Unfortunately, King was killed in 1968 before he could see his dream come true.

What do these words mean? You can use a dictionary.
segregation slavery non-violent protest speech rhythm

Race Riots

Not everyone believed in non-violent protest. In the 1960s there were race riots in many U.S. cities. Probably the worst riot was in Detroit. This is the riot that C.C. talks about in *Dreamgirls*. It started on 23rd July 1967 and lasted five days.

The Sounds of the Times

Black music changed very quickly during these years. Some artists used music to make political messages. Others just wanted their music to be popular with both white and black audiences.

1950s Jazz and the Blues were very popular sounds. Billie Holiday was a famous singer.

Billie Holiday

1960s Soul and R&B ('Rhythm & Blues') became very popular. Important artists at this time were James Brown and Aretha Franklin.

James Brown

The Jackson Five

1970s Disco arrived! Singers like Donna Summer and groups like the Jackson Five were big hits.

Do you know any singers / groups from the 1960s and 1970s? Do you like them? How are they different from singers / groups today?

Chapters 1–4

Before you read

1 Complete the sentences with these words.
You can use a dictionary.
pop charts disappointed stage talented recording contract back-up

- **a)** James is going to be a top tennis player, he's very … .
- **b)** When the singer walked onto the … , the crowd went wild.
- **c)** The new group have got a … with Happy Records.
- **d)** We were very … when we couldn't get tickets for the show.
- **e)** He isn't the lead singer, he sings … .
- **f)** Their song is now at number 10 on the … .

2 Choose the correct word. You can use a dictionary.

- **a)** That record label / album usually has great singers.
- **b)** How many songs are there on their new label / album?
- **c)** There were many civil rights marches / walks in the 1960s.

3 Look at People and Places on pages 4–5. Answer the questions.

- **a)** Who dreams of becoming a star?
- **b)** Who dreams of becoming a music manager?
- **c)** Who was the founder of the City of Detroit?
- **d)** Why is Detroit sometimes called the 'Motor City'?

After you read

4 Answer the questions.

- **a)** Who wins the talent contest?
- **b)** Why is Jimmy happy for the girls to sing back-up?
- **c)** Why do Curtis and C.C. talk to Jimmy?
- **d)** Who steals C.C.'s song *Cadillac Car*?
- **e)** How does *Steppin' to the Bad Side* become a hit?
- **f)** Why does Marty leave?

5 What do you think?

- **a)** Will Jimmy Early be more successful with Curtis as his manager?
- **b)** Will C.C. write more hit songs?
- **c)** What will happen between Curtis and Effie?

Chapters 5–8

Before you read

6 Match the two halves of the sentences. You can use a dictionary.

a)	He betrayed his sister	i)	but she doesn't work now.
b)	I couldn't persuade	ii)	when he told them her secret.
c)	She had a great career	iii)	drugs, they're bad for you.
d)	You should never take	iv)	the script for the new film.
e)	The producers sent him	v)	her to go to the party.

7 Complete the sentences with these words.
You can use a dictionary.

riots racist anniversary relationship audience

a) How many people are there tonight in the … ?
b) The police arrested a lot of people during the … .
c) Their … is very good. They're going to get married.
d) They only let white people in. They're very … .
e) It's our … today. We've been married twenty years.

After you read

8 Are the sentences true or false? Correct the false sentences.

a) The *American Bandstand* producer doesn't like the act.
b) Effie is happy for Deena to sing lead.
c) C.C. doesn't want to write songs about civil rights.
d) Curtis doesn't love Effie any more.
e) Effie decides herself to leave the group.
f) Deena and Curtis get married in Detroit.
g) Effie refuses to spend her brother's money.
h) Jimmy doesn't take drugs before the anniversary show.

9 What do you think?

a) What will happen to Jimmy now?
b) What will Effie do now that she is not in the group?
c) Will Rainbow Records continue to be successful?
d) Will Deena continue to do what Curtis tells her?

Chapters 9–12

Before you read

10 Guess which things will happen (✔)?
Which things won't happen (✗)?

a) Deena agrees to star in *Cleo*.
b) Something terrible happens to Jimmy.
c) Marty becomes Effie's manager.
d) Effie never again speaks to her brother.
e) Curtis steals a hit song from Effie.
f) Deena betrays Curtis to help Effie.
g) Deena finds out that Magic is Curtis's daughter.
h) Curtis goes to prison for bribery.

Now read chapters 9–12. Were your guesses correct?

After you read

11 Who says these things? Who are they speaking to?

a) 'The problem is you're too beautiful.'
b) 'You've taken all the feeling out of the song!'
c) 'Who are you?'
d) 'I've waited so long to hear that.'
e) 'You aren't a singer – you're my product.'
f) 'I want to get married and have kids.'
g) 'That man won't destroy our dreams again. Ever.'

12 Order the events.

a) Deena sends some important papers to Effie.
b) Curtis agrees to pay for Effie's record to avoid going to prison.
c) Curtis records Effie's song with a disco sound.
d) Effie sings with Deena and the Dreams at the goodbye concert.
e) Jimmy Early takes too many drugs and dies.
f) Effie, C.C. and Marty go to see Curtis with a lawyer.
g) C.C. writes a hit song for Effie.
h) Deena leaves Curtis.

13 What do you think?

a) What will happen to Deena, Lorrell and Effie in the future?
b) Will Curtis and Rainbow Records continue to be famous?